LAW AND ORDER

CHERRY LAKE Publishing

Published in the United States of America by Cherry Lake Publishing
Ann Arbor, Michigan
www.cherrylakepublishing.com

Content Adviser: Austin McCoy, Doctoral Candidate in History at the University of Michigan
Reading Adviser: Marla Conn MS, Ed., Literacy specialist, Read-Ability, Inc.

Photo Credits: © bikeriderlondon/Shutterstock, cover, 1, 15; © Rena Schild/Shutterstock, 5; © Paul Matthew Photography/ Shutterstock, 6; © EQRoy/Shutterstock, 9; © Brandon Bourdages/Shutterstock, 10; © SpeedKingz/Shutterstock, 12; © a katz/ Shutterstock, 16; © Junial Enterprises/Shutterstock, 17; © iofoto/Shutterstock, 18; © wavebreakmedia/Shutterstock, 20, 26; © Photographee.eu/Shutterstock, 23; © 1000 Words/Shutterstock, 24; © Ruslan Grumble/Shutterstock, 25; © Joseph Sohm/ Shutterstock, 28

Library of Congress Cataloging-in-Publication Data
Names: Mara, Wil, author.
Title: Law and order / Wil Mara.
Description: Ann Arbor : Cherry Lake Publishing, 2016. | Series: A citizen's guide |
    Includes bibliographical references and index.
Identifiers: LCCN 2016003906| ISBN 9781634710695 (hardcover) |
    ISBN 9781634711685 (pdf) | ISBN 9781634712675 (pbk.) | ISBN 9781634713665 (ebook)
Subjects: LCSH: Criminal justice, Administration of—United States—Juvenile literature.
Classification: LCC KF9223 .M27 2016 | DDC 364.973—dc23
LC record available at http://lccn.loc.gov/2016003906

Cherry Lake Publishing would like to acknowledge the work of the Partnership for 21st Century Learning.
Please visit www.p21.org for more information.

Printed in the United States of America
Corporate Graphics

ABOUT THE AUTHOR

Wil Mara is an award-winning and best-selling author of more than 150 books, many of which are educational titles for young readers. Further information about his work can be found at www.wilmara.com.

TABLE OF CONTENTS

The U.S. Constitution

Our country has been guided by a document called the Constitution for more than 200 years. The Constitution lays out the rules that our leaders use to run the nation. One of the most important of these rules sets down how our government is organized. There are three branches: the **legislative**, the **executive**, and the **judicial**. Each has its own responsibilities. The legislative branch is occupied by the U.S. Congress, whose primary function is to make laws. The executive branch oversees the daily administration of the country and is led by the president. And the judicial branch—charged with interpreting and applying the laws—is managed by the Supreme Court and the country's vast court system.

When America's Founding Fathers wrote the Constitution,

The Constitution outlines the priorities of the United States government.

The separation of powers ensures that the three branches are balanced.

they split the power structure of the government into three parts so that no one section would have absolute control. This approach, known as the **separation of powers**, provides a system of checks and balances. It means that running America is a shared responsibility.

The Constitution is divided into seven sections called articles, and Article III concerns itself with the government's judicial branch. It is shorter than the articles that describe the other two branches, yet the judiciary is just as powerful. It helps citizens resolve legal problems and determines appropriate punishments for those who have violated the law. The judicial branch also works to resolve conflicts between the other two branches of government.

Article III provides for a judicial body known as the Supreme Court. It is the most powerful court in the country. It usually has nine judges—also known as justices—and works out of Washington, D.C. Article III also allows for other, lower courts, which are found all over the country. The work these courts do on a daily basis is quite remarkable.

Life and Career Skills

Congress' greatest responsibility to the American people lies with its ability to create, adjust, or even withdraw existing laws. This means they basically write the "rule book" that U.S. citizens have to follow. Let's say you had all of Congress's power for a day. What one law would you get rid of? What one law would you create? Explain your thinking behind each of these decisions.

Courts

The Supreme Court is the highest-ranking body in the judicial branch. The only way an ordinary judge can become a member of the Supreme Court is by presidential appointment. Then the Senate must vote to confirm that person. This is not an automatic process. The Senate does not simply approve every person the president picks. The Senate holds hearings, and the person has to spend many demanding days answering questions from senators. Other people—both those in favor of the president's nominee and those who aren't—get the chance to speak their minds, too. This process can take several months. Since justices are appointed for life, the Senate wants to make sure it chooses the best people for the job.

The Supreme Court's job is to fairly and effectively interpret

In February 2016, when Justice Antonin Scalia passed away, crowds of people lined up at the Supreme Court to pay their respects to him.

the laws written for the United States. It's not an easy task. Justices have to understand what the creators of those laws had in mind when they created them. The process through which this happens takes the form of a court case. Lawyers on each side argue about the meaning and intent of a certain law. The case must go through other courts first before it can get to the Supreme Court. Those courts are much lower in rank and power. They have to offer their opinions about the case first before anyone can ask the Supreme Court to get involved. The Supreme Court receives requests to hear thousands of cases

EQUAL JUSTICE · UNDER · LAW ·

"Equal justice under law" means that the Supreme Court promises to decide each court case fairly for everyone.

every year. They agree to hear some, while most are rejected.

A federal court can only hear cases that fall within their **jurisdiction**. Mostly, federal courts deal with cases that involve the federal government. They also cover disputes between states, between a state and the federal government, or between the federal government and another country. There are federal courts located in every state. The states' courts are also organized into groups. These courts are called district courts, which hear general federal matters, and courts of **appeal**, which are obligated to review all appeals that are sent up from lower courts.

21st Century Content

Leadership is a quality found in many of America's greatest judges. Not all legal cases are "black and white," and that's because the language of the law isn't clear and simple. A good judge, however, will know how to navigate through these sticky situations when they arise. What specific characteristics do you think a person needs in order to be a good judge? Which of those characteristics do you believe you possess?

People who receive parking tickets can argue against them in court.

Federal court judges are also appointed by the president, with consent from the U.S. Senate. (The Senate is one of two chambers of the U.S. Congress—the other is the House of Representatives.)

Every state in the United States has its own set of courts, too. Their jurisdiction is limited to legal matters that concern their state. They deal with everything from parking tickets to homicide. They settle disputes concerning land ownership and cases of robbery or trespassing. They administer property distribution following someone's death. They also oversee marriages and divorces.

Just like federal courts, the state courts have several levels. At the top is a state supreme court. Below that there can be a tremendous variety of court levels depending on the state. In Texas, for example, there are five different court levels, while Illinois has only three. It is up to the state to decide how to organize its court structure, which is usually outlined in the state's constitution.

Judges, Juries, and Lawyers

There are two kinds of **trials** in the United States. A civil trial is when a person or group says that another has done something wrong to them. They get a lawyer and take the issue to court to let a judge—sometimes with the addition of a **jury**—decide the outcome of the case. A criminal trial is the other kind. This is where the government (local, state, or federal) charges that a law has been violated by a person or group of people. Thousands of trials of both types take place in the country every year.

A judge is a very important person in the U.S. court system and is highly respected. When court is in session, he or she will often be addressed as "Your Honor" or "The Honorable" (and then the judge's name). Judges are often referred to in these ways

Sometimes a jury determines the outcome of a trial.

when they're not in court, too. A judge's neighbors may choose to address them in this way when passing him or her on the street.

While some judges are appointed to their positions, others are elected just like many other government officials. Elected judges will have limited terms in their position, such as two or four years. Then they must publicly **campaign** for that position again. It is common for state judges, for example, to be elected rather than appointed.

Judges perform many tasks and are usually extremely busy people. For example, they have to review every request from police

Usually, police need search warrants before they can look through someone's house.

to issue a **search warrant**, which gives the police legal permission to search private property. During a trial, the judge is in charge of procedure and has to assure that everything runs smoothly. The judge will also decide minor matters such as the time when the trial begins and when everyone involved can break for lunch. The judge maintains order in the courtroom with the help of the **bailiff**. Judges have to be careful to stay within the limits of the law during any trial. Otherwise, one of the lawyers involved in the case may request a **mistrial** and be granted a new one.

Judges need to know how to keep a courtroom running smoothly.

A team of lawyers might need to do a lot of research and planning before a difficult case.

A judge also settles any matters where lawyers on opposing sides disagree. For example, the lawyers may disagree about who should be allowed to testify. The judge will listen to both sides of the argument, then decide if the person in question is allowed to speak. In a criminal trial, a judge has to ensure that a defendant—no matter how horrible the crime he or she is accused of—receives a fair and speedy trial. This is guaranteed by the Sixth Amendment of the Constitution. A judge may also decide on appropriate punishment when a defendant is found guilty.

A jury is a group of citizens chosen to hear a case and then render a **verdict**. The average size of a jury can run from eight to 12 people. The jury members receive instructions from time to time from the judge presiding over the case. They listen carefully to all the **evidence**, and afterward they meet alone and determine the verdict. Sometimes a jury is unable to reach a firm decision. When a hung jury happens, the entire case may begin again with new people chosen.

Any adult citizen can be picked for **jury duty**. Usually people are informed by a letter in the mail. People on jury duty have to

21st Century Content

Part of being a good lawyer in the United States requires choosing a certain point of view on a legal issue and then throwing your hard work and your reputation behind it. And in the world of law, that means being challenged by lawyers who disagree with you. Think about some legal issues that you feel strongly about. How far would you go to defend your beliefs? How sure are you that your beliefs are the right ones?

Some lawyers may specialize in real estate, divorce, or other types of law.

miss work in order to serve. Sometimes they lose their pay at their regular jobs while doing this service (although if a juror works for 10 days, after that he or she can receive $50 per day). Missing work upsets some people very much. However, the American court system cannot function without citizens performing this important duty.

Trials require the service of lawyers. There are hundreds of thousands of lawyers in the United States, most specializing in a certain area of law, such as real estate, copyright, divorce, or criminal. Whatever kind of trial it is, lawyers do most of the talking. They work to protect their client, with the ultimate goal of steering the case toward a favorable verdict. They speak to the judge and jury at the beginning of the case to tell their side of the issue. They question witnesses. They ask the judge to rule on issues that arise during the proceedings. At the end of the trial, the lawyers again speak to the jury in an attempt to sway them in their favor.

Once all the facts are presented and the argument phase is over, the lawyers can only sit and wait for the verdict. It can be a very stressful and demanding job, often with a client's entire future hanging in the balance.

Life and Career Skills

Public elections for judges are held on a regular basis, and you will have the right to cast your vote for these judges as soon as you reach voting age. Judges can have terms usually ranging from two to four years. Do you feel these terms are just the right length of time, or should they be longer or shorter? Explain your reasoning.

The Role of Law Enforcement

Police officers, detectives, sheriffs, and other law enforcement officials play a big role in court cases. If a crime is committed, they look for evidence and other critical clues in an attempt to find the guilty party. They may call in other specialists, such as forensic pathologists, who examine evidence such as blood spatter and footprints. Then they have to seek out and arrest the **suspects**. During a trial, these officials may be required to testify for lawyers on one side of the case or the other.

The federal government has different types of law enforcement professionals. One of the most familiar is the Federal Bureau of Investigation, or FBI. The FBI is responsible for investigating more than 200 different types of crime, such as bank robberies, kidnappings, and **cyberterrorism**. Crimes that violate state or local

Cyberterrorists sometimes target government networks.

The Secret Service accompanies the president on trips.

laws, like driving offenses, shoplifting, and most murders, are handled by the state or local police. The FBI's headquarters is in Quantico, Virginia, but it has offices all around the nation.

Other federal law enforcement groups you may know include the Secret Service and the U.S. Postal Inspectors. The Secret Service protects the president, vice president, their families, and visiting heads of state. Agents also investigate cases of **counterfeiting** and falsified credit cards. Postal inspectors investigate crimes where the mail system, telephone, or Internet

The Secret Service investigates counterfeit money.

People who testify in court have to swear to tell "the truth, the whole truth, and nothing but the truth."

was used. One example of this is the "get rich quick" schemes that convince people to send money through the mail or through online accounts for investments that don't exist.

Just as the federal government has special groups that enforce the law and investigate crimes, so do states, counties, cities, and towns. Wherever you live, you live under the protection of a local police force. Sometimes they walk around making sure cars are legally parked. On another day, they might be investigating a robbery or a murder. In college towns, there are often police who

Life and Career Skills

In 1963, a man named Ernesto Miranda was arrested in Arizona. Police asked him many questions at the time of the arrest. At his trial, the answers Miranda gave formed the only evidence **prosecutors** had to use against him. He was convicted and sentenced to a jail term of up to 30 years. When the Supreme Court reviewed the case later on, it decided to overturn Miranda's conviction because the police had failed to inform him that he did not have to answer their questions. This was a violation of Miranda's Fifth Amendment rights. As a result of this case, in 1966, all law enforcement officials became required to give any captured suspect a "Miranda warning," which informs them of their right to remain silent so anything they say will not be used against them in a court of law. Do you feel this is fair, or do you think Miranda's on-the-spot confession should have been considered valid evidence?

The Black Lives Matter movement began in 2013.

deal specifically with problems on campus. Whatever the case, there will come a time when all these professionals will be asked to testify in a courtroom in an attempt to determine the truth. They want those who are guilty to pay for the crimes they've committed.

21st Century Content

The main job of the police is to protect the local citizens. But what happens when they fail at this? In the 2010s, several high-profile cases of police officers shooting unarmed suspects rocked the United States. The majority of these victims were young black men and in 2013, three activists started a movement called Black Lives Matter in order to raise awareness about this issue. The movement has gained popularity all over the country with supporters attending protests and posting on social media.

Think About It

Ask your parents or teachers if they have ever been interviewed for jury duty.
Did they get chosen to serve on the case? What was the experience like?

Would you rather be a) a police officer, b) a lawyer, or c) a politician? Think
about how each one makes decisions to interpret laws in their daily work.
Which skills do they need? Which of those skills do you have?

[21ST CENTURY SKILLS LIBRARY]

For More Information

BOOKS

Krull, Kathleen, and Anna DiVito (illustrator). *A Kid's Guide to America's Bill of Rights*. New York: HarperCollins, 2015.

Steinkraus, Kyla. *The Constitution*. Vero Beach, FL: Rourke, 2015.

Winter, Jonah, and Barry Blitt (illustrator). *The Founding Fathers! The Horse-Ridin', Fiddle-Playin', Book-Readin', Gun-Totin' Gentlemen Who Started America*. New York: Atheneum, 2015.

ON THE WEB

Congress for Kids—The Supreme Court
www.congressforkids.net/Judicialbranch_supremecourt.htm

Kids.gov—Government
https://kids.usa.gov/government/index.shtml

PBS Kids—The Democracy Project: How Does Government Affect Me?
http://pbskids.org/democracy/my-government/

GLOSSARY

appeal (uh-PEEL) a case that asks a higher court to review a lower court's legal decision

bailiff (BAY-lif) an official in a court of law who maintains order in the court

campaign (kam-PAYN) to take an organized action in order to achieve a particular goal

counterfeiting (KOUN-tur-fit-ing) faking something but looking almost exactly like the real thing

cyberterrorism (SYE-bur-TER-uh-RIZ-uhm) the politically motivated use of computers to intentionally cause severe disruption and widespread fear in society

evidence (EV-ih-duhns) information and facts that help prove something is true or not true

executive (ig-ZEK-yuh-tiv) branch of the federal government that is headed by the president

judicial (joo-DISH-uhl) branch of the federal government that is made up of the court system

jurisdiction (joor-es-DIK-shuhn) the limits within which a certain authority may be exercised

jury (JOOR-ee) a group of people, usually 12 in number, who listen to the facts at a trial and decide whether the accused person is guilty or not guilty

jury duty (JOOR-ee DOO-tee) the obligation of a citizen to serve on a jury

legislative (LEJ-is-lay-tiv) branch of the federal government that is made up of Congress

mistrial (MIS-trye-uhl) a trial that has no legal effect because of some error that happened during the proceedings

prosecutors (PRAH-sih-kyoo-turz) lawyers who represent the government in criminal trials

search warrant (SURCH WOR-uhnt) an order from a court that allows the police to enter and search a place

separation of powers (sep-uh-RAY-shuhn of POU-urz) the system in place so that executive, judicial, and legislative decisions are made by different people

suspects (SUHS-spekts) people who are thought to have committed crimes

trials (TRYE-uhlz) examinations of evidence in courts of law to decide if charges or claims are true

verdict (VUR-dikt) the decision of a jury on whether an accused person is guilty or not

INDEX